Just Fine the Way They Are

From Dirt Roads to Rail Roads to Interstates

Connie Nordhielm Wooldridge

Illustrated by **Richard Walz**

CALKINS CREEK

HONESDALE, PENNSYLVANIA

ACKNOWLEDGMENTS

Thanks to Joseph Jarzen, executive director of the Indiana National Road Association, and to Jim Harlan, executive director of the Wayne County Historical Museum, Richmond, Indiana.

—*C.N.W.*

ISBN: 978-1-59078-710-6

Library of Congress Control Number: 2010929539

CALKINS CREEK
An Imprint of Boyds Mills Press, Inc.
815 Church Street
Honesdale, Pennsylvania 18431

10 9 8 7 6 5 4 3 2 1

CPSIA facility code: BP 306219

To my dad, Berndt Nordhielm, who drove a Chevy along the roads of Ohio, Indiana, and Illinois with my mom riding shotgun and me in the backseat . . . carsick —C.N.W.

For Kit and J. C. Smith, new relatives and new friends —R.W.

Mr. John Slack, the tavern keeper, was not happy. He was not happy at all. The year was 1805, and two high-minded senators—one from Ohio and one from Connecticut—were telling the U.S. Congress that the United States needed a National Road so the folks who lived in the East could get to the Ohio River. According to these two fancy-talking senators, a National Road would cement the Union and "make the crooked ways straight, and the rough ways smooth."

The trouble was, the road they had in mind would pass right by John Slack's tavern at the top of Laurel Hill in Pennsylvania, and John Slack liked the dirt road that was already there just fine. Wagon drivers would stay the night at his tavern when their wagons got stuck in the mud coming up the hill. They'd spend the next day digging out and bed down at his tavern for another night. Same thing would happen on the return trip. The way John Slack saw it, a good road was bad for business, and he wanted none of it! Things were just fine the way they were.

But Congress went and built the National Road anyway. And did the dang thing stop when it reached the Ohio River in 1816? No sir, it did not! By 1833, the Road stretched all the way to Columbus, Ohio. Then it kept going till it crossed Indiana and half of Illinois to the capital city of Vandalia where, in 1839, it stopped dead in its tracks.

It stopped because of arguments over money and about which way it should go from there—and because of the small fact that the capital of Illinois was no longer in Vandalia; it had up and moved to Springfield. So there was no reason for the Road to be where it had gotten itself.

But most folks didn't agree with John Slack's bad opinion of the National Road. Most folks thought it was a real fine thing. They thought it was the Main Street of America, where ideas and people and things to sell moved back and forth across the country.

Living near the National Road was pure excitement. Little boys watched huge Conestoga wagons—long lines of them—pass through their towns carrying freight. They went to bed dreaming of driving one of those very wagons when they grew up. Or they dreamed of driving one of the stagecoaches that carried people and mail. When a little boy looked out his window, it seemed to him as if the sun itself traveled the Road every day from east to west.

But in 1830—even before the National Road was completed—one of the owners of the National Road Stage Company was not happy. No sir. Mr. Lucius Stockton was not happy at all. In the early summer of that year, an enterprising tinkerer by the name of Peter Cooper ran a newfangled invention called a steam locomotive over two steel rails at the speed of fifteen miles per hour. The locomotive pulled a car behind it carrying the directors of the Baltimore and Ohio Railroad. Peter Cooper named his locomotive the *Tom Thumb,* and he bragged that it could chug up and down hills and around curves as slick as a whistle.

But the question was, Who needed a "rail" road when there was a National Road? Who needed a steam locomotive when horses were already doing the job? Lucius Stockton decided it was time to show Peter Cooper and his locomotive that things were just fine the way they were. Lucius Stockton told Peter Cooper a horse could pull a car full of passengers along the rails better than any old *Tom Thumb*, and he would prove it in a race.

So Peter Cooper hitched his *Tom Thumb* to a car on one set of tracks and Lucius Stockton hitched his best gray horse to a car on another, and off they went. Each car carried a load of passengers who shouted insults at the folks in the car on the other tracks. The gray took an early lead. But then steam began to blow out of the *Tom Thumb*, and the locomotive passed the horse. Lucius Stockton's heart sank, but the race wasn't over yet.

A band inside the engine of the *Tom Thumb* slipped. The locomotive gasped for breath and lost speed. Victory went to Lucius Stockton and his gray horse. That would show Peter Cooper and the Baltimore and Ohio Railroad that things were just fine the way they were.

But many folks didn't agree with Lucius Stockton's bad opinion of the railroad. They thought gliding along in a passenger train was a real fine thing. A celebrated Georgia man said that being jolted along over a road full of potholes was behind the times.

A band inside the engine of the *Tom Thumb* slipped. The locomotive gasped for breath and lost speed. Victory went to Lucius Stockton and his gray horse. That would show Peter Cooper and the Baltimore and Ohio Railroad that things were just fine the way they were.

But many folks didn't agree with Lucius Stockton's bad opinion of the railroad. They thought gliding along in a passenger train was a real fine thing. A celebrated Georgia man said that being jolted along over a road full of potholes was behind the times.

In 1851, Stockton's coach line was moved off the National Road. Poems were written about how the new locomotives were bringing the Road to a sad end: "For the Steam King rules the traveled world," one poet said. "And the Old Pike's left to die."

Yes sir, the National Road's work was done. Its day was over. By 1899, little boys were watching steam locomotives fly by and dreaming of being train engineers when they grew up. The National Road turned into a dirt path used by a few farmers to haul their goods to town.

But those very farmers were not happy. They were not happy at all. The Road might have been sad-looking and full of potholes and weeds, but it pretty much belonged to them. And then here came these citified dandies riding down the road on contraptions called bicycles. These "wheelmen" claimed the act of walking was on its last legs! They scared the horses and ran over people when they lost control of their machines, which was frequently. And then they started demanding that Congress build better, smoother roads for them to ride on. Why should the taxes of honest, hardworking folks go to build a smooth road for a doggone bicycle?

But even worse things were coming. In 1908, Henry Ford's first
Model T automobile appeared. It was a personal mobility machine
that could go places a train couldn't. And with his assembly line,
Henry Ford could make cars so cheaply, anyone could afford one.
Then, of course, these pesky new automobile owners joined the wheelmen,
and pretty soon everybody and his mother were hollering for better roads.
   Again.
   Hogwash was what the farmers said. The roads were good enough
for a horse and wagon, and everybody else could take the train!
Things were just fine the way they were.

Most Americans didn't agree. They were tired of crowded train stations with routes and schedules that bossed them around and told them where they could go and when they could go there. They wanted to hop into their shiny new automobiles and go wherever they wanted. But they couldn't do that unless they had good roads to travel.

Pretty soon everybody who was crying out for better roads banded together into a highway lobby that could talk to Congress with one great, big voice. The automobile makers joined the lobby. The folks in the oil industry did, too. So did the cement makers and the steelmakers and folks in small towns who were excited about what the roads might bring to the out-of-the-way places where they lived. In 1912, Congress voted to spend money for a national highway system that would include the National Road.

By the 1920s, the hollering for good roads had sparked a bigger idea.
Roads should be connected and numbered so people could follow the
numbers and get where they wanted to go. The Old National Road, now
paved and smooth, became U.S. 40, part of a route that ran clear across the
country—more than three thousand miles—from Atlantic City, New Jersey,
in the East to San Francisco, California, in the West.

US
40

By the 1950s, the military folks joined the hollering for good roads. They needed to be able to move from place to place fast if they were going to defend the nation. Why should they have to stop at stop signs in towns and cities they only wanted to pass by on their way to somewhere else? Congress decided to build a whole new system of roads, right next to the old roads, that would have entrances and exits and no stop signs. That way, military vehicles, along with regular old cars and trucks, could get where they wanted to go even faster.

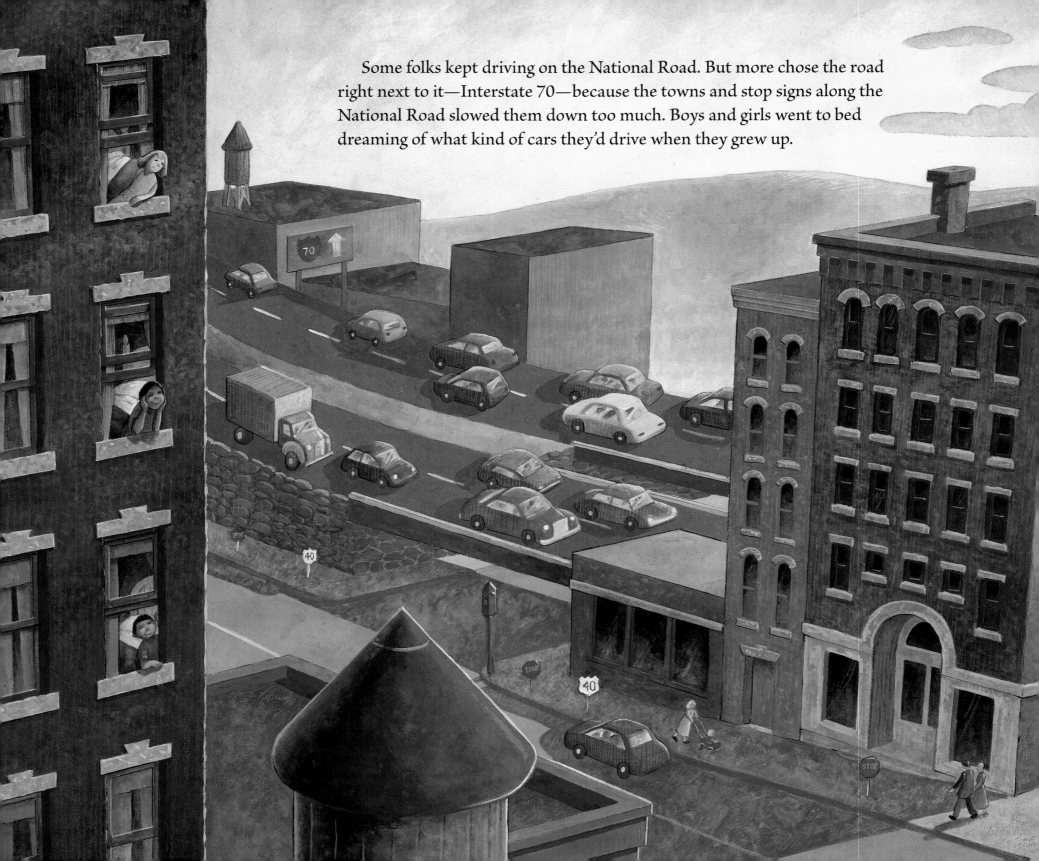

Some folks kept driving on the National Road. But more chose the road right next to it—Interstate 70—because the towns and stop signs along the National Road slowed them down too much. Boys and girls went to bed dreaming of what kind of cars they'd drive when they grew up.

By the end of the 1900s, most everyone had a car, and some had two or three. And all over the country, there were roads like spaghetti that could get a person just about anywhere. So this story should be ending with a "happily ever after."

But it doesn't. Because instead of a "happily ever after," what do we get but a bunch of folks spoiling everything, saying all those cars and all those roads might not be such a good thing . . . saying there might be an end to how much oil can be pulled out of the earth to make into gasoline . . . saying that cars are dirtying up the breathing air down here where we live and causing trouble we can only guess at way high up in the atmosphere.

And *then* what do we get but a pack of crazy thinkers coming up with ideas about how to make cars run on things like electricity and fuel cells and even corn. Next thing they'll be saying is we don't even *need* cars or roads anymore because they've come up with something better.

All of which is plain nonsense. Because things are just fine the way they are. . . .

TIMELINE

1806 The U.S. House of Representatives votes in favor of a federally funded road connecting Cumberland, Maryland, to the Ohio River. (Southern representatives object because they insist it's a *northern* road, not a *national* road.)

1811 Construction of the National Road begins.

1816 The National Road reaches Wheeling (later part of West Virginia) on the Ohio River, and the government's goal of providing a connection between the settled East and the river systems of the Midwest is realized. Senator John C. Calhoun argues that the Road should continue its westward journey.

1829 Peter Cooper moves to Baltimore and begins work on an experimental small locomotive called the *Tom Thumb*.

1830 Even as new sections of the Road are built, older sections fall into disrepair. Congress begins to turn the administration and maintenance of the Road over to the states, and tollhouses are built to collect money to help with the expense. The *Tom Thumb* races a railroad car pulled by a horse and is defeated.

1832 More than 190,000 head of livestock pass the tollhouse in Zanesville, Ohio, and forty to one hundred wagons a day pass through Richmond, Indiana.

1833 The Road is completed to Columbus, Ohio.

1839 The Road reaches Vandalia, Illinois. Further building is halted because the U.S. Congress cannot agree on the route.

1845 The first steel rails for tracks are manufactured in Danville, Pennsylvania.

1851 The Good Intent and Stockton stagecoach lines are no longer allowed on the National Road.

1853 The Baltimore and Ohio Railroad reaches Wheeling. Traffic along the Road declines.

1880 Bicyclists organize into the League of American Wheelmen and demand better roads.

1900 The United States is almost completely connected by rail. The first automobile show in America is held in New York City.

1908 Henry Ford's first Model T rolls off the assembly line.

1921 The Federal Aid Highway Act shifts the focus from local roads to a connected system of highways.

1960s Railroad companies declare bankruptcy.

2004 The national newspaper *USA Today* reports that traffic problems are getting worse faster than they can be fixed.

And *then* what do we get but a pack of crazy thinkers coming up with ideas about how to make cars run on things like electricity and fuel cells and even corn. Next thing they'll be saying is we don't even *need* cars or roads anymore because they've come up with something better.

All of which is plain nonsense. Because things are just fine the way they are. . . .

TIMELINE

1806 The U.S. House of Representatives votes in favor of a federally funded road connecting Cumberland, Maryland, to the Ohio River. (Southern representatives object because they insist it's a *northern* road, not a *national* road.)

1811 Construction of the National Road begins.

1816 The National Road reaches Wheeling (later part of West Virginia) on the Ohio River, and the government's goal of providing a connection between the settled East and the river systems of the Midwest is realized. Senator John C. Calhoun argues that the Road should continue its westward journey.

1829 Peter Cooper moves to Baltimore and begins work on an experimental small locomotive called the *Tom Thumb*.

1830 Even as new sections of the Road are built, older sections fall into disrepair. Congress begins to turn the administration and maintenance of the Road over to the states, and tollhouses are built to collect money to help with the expense. The *Tom Thumb* races a railroad car pulled by a horse and is defeated.

1832 More than 190,000 head of livestock pass the tollhouse in Zanesville, Ohio, and forty to one hundred wagons a day pass through Richmond, Indiana.

1833 The Road is completed to Columbus, Ohio.

1839 The Road reaches Vandalia, Illinois. Further building is halted because the U.S. Congress cannot agree on the route.

1845 The first steel rails for tracks are manufactured in Danville, Pennsylvania.

1851 The Good Intent and Stockton stagecoach lines are no longer allowed on the National Road.

1853 The Baltimore and Ohio Railroad reaches Wheeling. Traffic along the Road declines.

1880 Bicyclists organize into the League of American Wheelmen and demand better roads.

1900 The United States is almost completely connected by rail. The first automobile show in America is held in New York City.

1908 Henry Ford's first Model T rolls off the assembly line.

1921 The Federal Aid Highway Act shifts the focus from local roads to a connected system of highways.

1960s Railroad companies declare bankruptcy.

2004 The national newspaper *USA Today* reports that traffic problems are getting worse faster than they can be fixed.

BIBLIOGRAPHY

Books

Carson, Iain, and Vijay V. Vaitheeswaran. *Zoom: The Global Race to Fuel the Car of the Future*. New York: Twelve, 2007. This book looks into the future and imagines what the next chapter of the story of cars and roads might be.

Hulbert, Archer Butler. *The Cumberland Road*. Reprint of 1902–1905 edition. New York: AMS Press, 1971. Archer Butler Hulbert, who died in 1933, was a history professor with a keen interest in transportation. From 1905 to 1914, he worked for the U.S. Office of Public Roads and lectured on the economics of good roads.

Hungerford, Edward. *The Story of the Baltimore & Ohio Railroad, 1827–1927*. Vol. 1. New York: G. P. Putnam's Sons, 1928. This book was written in the years when railroads were still booming. It includes the history of Peter Cooper's locomotive, the *Tom Thumb*.

Raitz, Karl, ed. *The National Road* and *A Guide to the National Road*. Baltimore: Johns Hopkins University Press, 1996.

Schneider, Norris F. *The National Road: Main Street of America*. Columbus: Ohio Historical Society, 1975. Short pamphlets published by historical societies (such as this one) provide brief, accurate summaries of large topics. This pamphlet contains many old maps and photos.

Searight, Thomas B. *The Old Pike*. Orange, VA: Green Tree Press, 1971. Thomas Searight was born in 1827. His father and grandfather owned taverns on the National Road. He wrote this book in 1894, because he was afraid the railroads would wipe the National Road out of public memory. Joseph E. Morse and R. Duff Green edited, illustrated, and republished the book in 1971.

Web Sites*

The National Road originally passed through five states (after the Civil War, West Virginia became the sixth), and each has a Web site:

• Illinois: nationalroad.org

• Indiana: indiananationalroad.org

• Maryland: marylandnationalroad.org

• Ohio: ohionationalroad.org

• Pennsylvania: nationalroadpa.org

• West Virginia: historicwvnationalroad.org

*Web sites active at time of publication

PLACES TO VISIT

Baltimore and Ohio Railroad Museum
901 West Pratt Street
Baltimore, Maryland 21223
(410) 752-2490
borail.org*
Houses railcars pulled by horses, an extensive collection of nineteenth-century steam locomotives, and a replica of the *Tom Thumb*.

Fort Necessity/National Road Interpretive and Education Center
1 Washington Parkway
Farmington, Pennsylvania 15437
(724) 329-5512

Huddleston Farmhouse and the National Road Interpretive Center
838 National Road, Mount Auburn
Cambridge City, Indiana 47327
(765) 478-3172
www.indianalandmarks.org/?50185bf0
Huddleston represents a slice of life along the Road during the 1840s; the center tells the story of the entire Road.

National Road and Toll House
14302 National Highway
  LaVale, Maryland 21502
    (301) 777-5132
      mdmountainside.com/attraction.php?attraction=160
        Features a seven-sided toll-gate house first constructed in 1835.

National Road Interpretive Center
106 South 5th Street
Vandalia, Illinois 62471
(618) 283-9380

National Road/Zane Grey Museum
8850 East Pike
Norwich, Ohio 43767
(740) 872-3143; (800) 752-2602
ohsweb.ohiohistory.org/places/se07/
Contains a 136-foot diorama of the National Road.

Vandalia State House
315 West Gallatin Street
Vandalia, Illinois 62471
(618) 283-1161

Wayne County Historical Museum
1150 North A Street
Richmond, Indiana 47374
(765) 962-5756
waynecountyhistoricalmuseum.com
Includes a covered wagon, fourteen vintage automobiles that were manufactured locally, and an airplane.

Web sites active at time of publication